ARCHAEOLOGY

by
PAUL DEVEREUX

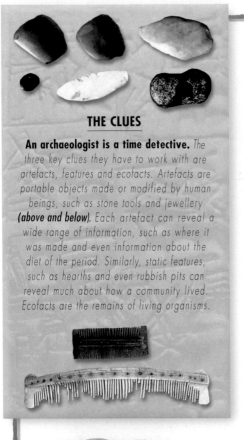

THE CLUES

An archaeologist is a time detective. *The three key clues they have to work with are artefacts, features and ecofacts. Artefacts are portable objects made or modified by human beings, such as stone tools and jewellery (**above and below**). Each artefact can reveal a wide range of information, such as where it was made and even information about the diet of the period. Similarly, static features, such as hearths and even rubbish pits can reveal much about how a community lived. Ecofacts are the remains of living organisms.*

WHAT IS ARCHAEOLOGY?

Archaeology is the study of the physical remains of the human past. It helps to tell us who we are, and where we came from. Modern archaeology began at the end of the 17th century in Britain, when it became fashionable for country gentlemen to study visible ancient monuments like Stonehenge. In the 19th century, people began investigating suspected archaeological sites. At first this was done crudely and carelessly, but gradually digging transformed into precise excavation, and the interpretation of finds improved. Since then, science has revolutionized archaeology.

PLANTS IN THE PAST

Plant remains are an important source of archaeological information. All flowering plants produce pollen (*right*), the grains of which are virtually indestructible. These little time capsules can tell us whether a site was hot, cold, dry or wet, for example. Plant remains can tell an archaeologist what crops were grown at the time, what foods were eaten and even what herbal medicines may have been used. The recovery, identification and analysis of plant remains is called 'archaeobotany'.

ANCIENT ADVENTURE

Modern archaeologists are scientists, heroes of the mind rather than colourful adventurers like the fictional archaeologist Indiana Jones (*left*). Nevertheless, field archaeologists can occasionally find themselves in frightening situations. In the 1990s, a group searching for a lost Mayan city in a Central American jungle were captured by guerrillas. Fortunately, they were eventually released unharmed.

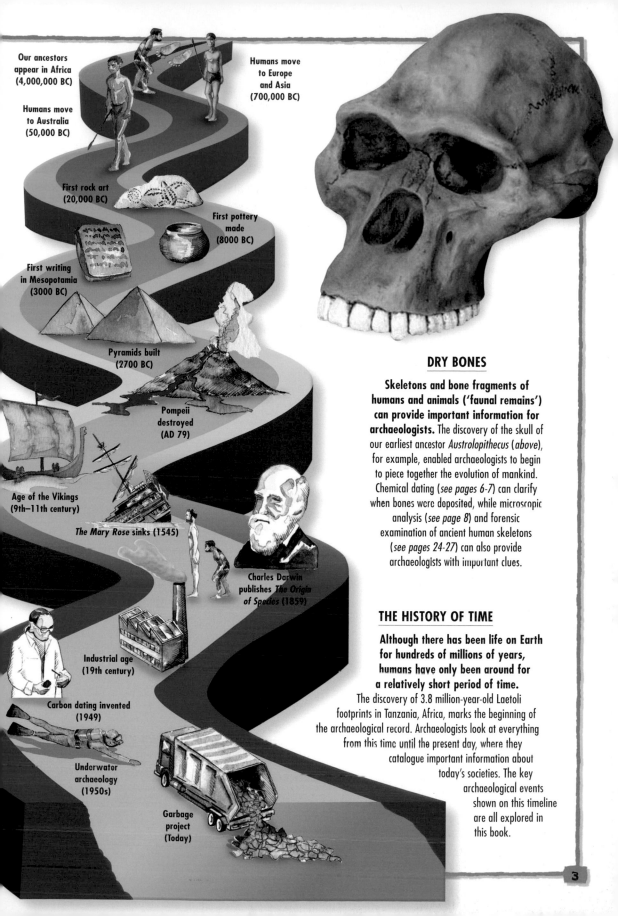

Our ancestors appear in Africa (4,000,000 BC)

Humans move to Europe and Asia (700,000 BC)

Humans move to Australia (50,000 BC)

First rock art (20,000 BC)

First pottery made (8000 BC)

First writing in Mesopotamia (3000 BC)

Pyramids built (2700 BC)

Pompeii destroyed (AD 79)

Age of the Vikings (9th–11th century)

The Mary Rose sinks (1545)

Charles Darwin publishes *The Origin of Species* (1859)

Industrial age (19th century)

Carbon dating invented (1949)

Underwater archaeology (1950s)

Garbage project (Today)

DRY BONES

Skeletons and bone fragments of humans and animals ('faunal remains') can provide important information for archaeologists. The discovery of the skull of our earliest ancestor *Austrolopithecus* (*above*), for example, enabled archaeologists to begin to piece together the evolution of mankind. Chemical dating (*see pages 6-7*) can clarify when bones were deposited, while microscopic analysis (*see page 8*) and forensic examination of ancient human skeletons (*see pages 24-27*) can also provide archaeologists with important clues.

THE HISTORY OF TIME

Although there has been life on Earth for hundreds of millions of years, humans have only been around for a relatively short period of time. The discovery of 3.8 million-year-old Laetoli footprints in Tanzania, Africa, marks the beginning of the archaeological record. Archaeologists look at everything from this time until the present day, where they catalogue important information about today's societies. The key archaeological events shown on this timeline are all explored in this book.

If an archaeologist has a rough idea where buried artefacts might be found, he can use a metal detector. These detect where metal artefacts or jewellery are buried.

An auger is a corkscrew-like device with a T-shaped handle that can be rotated to bore into the ground. It can detect hollow areas underground, which may be something of archaeological interest.

Because excavation destroys a site, it is crucial to keep records when on a dig. Archaeologists plot the exact position of each object. Soil that is swept up during a dig is sieved to check for tiny bones or objects that might have been missed. Some soil is placed in water, as seeds and other remains will float to the surface.

Once the archaeological layer is exposed, people carefully use trowels and fine brushes to scrape away the soil. To reveal really delicate objects, dental probes are often used.

Ancient artefacts and bones are often extremely delicate, and must be excavated with great care. This archaeologist is carefully removing soil particles with a fine brush.

TRICKS & TECHNIQUES: INVESTIGATING A SITE

Archaeologists have gradually developed a large armoury of techniques to help them find and survey sites. Many are very basic, while others require the use of scientific equipment. Once a suspected site has been discovered, excavation begins. A plan of a site is created, and the archaeologist then decides where best to cut exploratory trenches. These can be arranged on a grid layout so the exact locations of finds can be plotted. When excavating, layers are exposed in trench walls, like slices of cake.

Archaeologists can also preview archaeological sites by studying aerial photographs. Ground disturbed in the past tends to hold moisture better than undisturbed land. This affects the vegetation, and dark crop markings are clearly visible from the air. Buried foundations or roads usually produce light crop markings.

Fieldwalking involves systematically walking over ploughed fields, scouring the ground for fragments of pottery, worked flints and other signs of human activity. Any finds are then plotted on a grid, so archaeologists can decide on the best places to start excavating.

Instruments called magnometers and gradiometers can be used to measure magnetic variations in the ground, which may indicate an archaeological site. Ground radar can often give a picture of an underground structure where many other methods just give a 'beep'. Results are usually displayed on a screen or printout. Ground radar will detect a range of targets including metals, plastics, ceramics and others.

magnometer

gradiometer

ground radar

Resistivity meters are used to measure moisture. Solid ground retains more moisture (low resistivity) than buried building foundations, roads or stone structures (high resistivity). A resistivity meter is attached to electrodes inserted into the ground. An electric current is then passed into the soil, which gives a moisture reading.

DATING TECHNIQUES

There are several dating techniques that can be used for archaeological purposes. These include processes such as the use of typology, which matches an artefact's style to a period, and dendrochronology, which involves examining tree trunks. There are also a series of more complex chemical dating processes. These techniques can tell an archaeologist exactly how old something is by measuring carbon, minerals or levels of radiation.

DENDROCHRONOLOGY

Dendrochronology is the technique of dating by tree rings. A tree trunk is built up in concentric rings, each representing a year's growth. These can be counted to reveal how old a tree is. Tree-ring dating has yielded some very precise dates. For example, by studying the timbers found at a Bronze Age settlement site at Cortaillod-Est in Switzerland, archaeologists were able to determine that the community was established with four houses in 1010 BC, expanded four times in subsequent years, and that a fence was added in 985 BC!

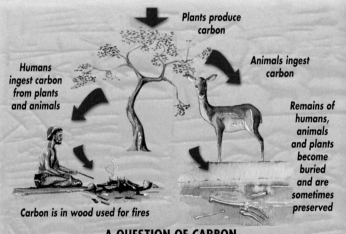

Plants produce carbon

Humans ingest carbon from plants and animals

Animals ingest carbon

Remains of humans, animals and plants become buried and are sometimes preserved

Carbon is in wood used for fires

A QUESTION OF CARBON

All forms of life on Earth take in and store carbon from plants – a process that stops at death. As carbon decays at a known rate, the amount left in an organic sample can reveal how long ago it died. Archaeologists use a technique called radiocarbon dating to measure the amount of carbon left in a sample, and thus find out from when it dates. Geiger counters or the more advanced Accelerator Mass Spectrometry machines are used to measure radiocarbon content.

VOLCANIC CLUES

Potassium-argon dating works by measuring the rate of decay of potassium in volcanic rock. It is useful at early human sites in volcanic countries, where our earliest ancestors laid down their footprints in cooling volcanic ash (*see above and pages 10-11*). Potassium-argon dating established exactly when these footprints were made.

STYLE SLEUTHS

Styles have always changed over time, and different cultures have different styles. In the same way as we can tell the difference in style between a car produced today and a car produced in 1924, so archaeologists can sort out the time-groupings of pots, stone axes and other artefacts. This technique is called typological sequencing.

URANIUM-SERIES DATING

This technique is invaluable for dating caves, and showing the order in which a cave was occupied or used. It is used to date rocks rich in calcium carbonate, such as stalactites and stalagmites. Archaeologists often use this technique because it can date back further than radiocarbon dating. The technique was used to date this cave dwelling in Cappadocia, Turkey.

ARTEFACTS & ARCHAEOLOGISTS

UNDER THE MICROSCOPE

Archaeologists can use microscopes to find out more about a site. At Skara Brae, a group of Neolithic stone-built houses on the Scottish Orkney Islands dating from 3000 BC, stone and shell cups were found with residues in them. Microscopic analysis revealed traces of milk and cereal products, casting light on the diet of the people of the time. Traces of red ochre have also been discovered, indicating ritual activity.

Artefacts are objects discovered in excavations, often made of clay, stone or metal. They are usually the most plentiful links to the past for archaeologists, as they tend to survive far longer than bone fragments or plant remains. However, when clues are not immediately obvious, there are a range of more complicated, scientific techniques that can be used to unravel the past. These range from chemical etching and microscopic analysis to DNA profiling and the use of computers and laser plotters.

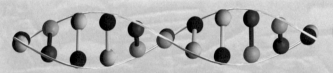

SECRETS OF LIFE

DNA is the blueprint of life for all living things. It is a secret code of special instructions that makes every plant and animal distinct from one another, and from other species. It is also a valuable tool for archaeologists. At Cuddle Springs in Australia, 30,000-year-old stone tools analysed under an electron microscope revealed traces of blood and hair. DNA analysis revealed the traces to be from a kangaroo, proving that the people of the time were able to hunt large animals.

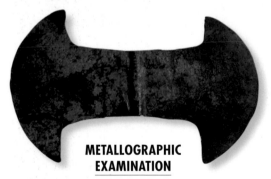

METALLOGRAPHIC EXAMINATION

This technique involves using chemicals to strip away a polished section from a metal artefact to reveal the metal structure below. The area can then be studied under a microscope. This can disclose the methods used to make an artefact. It can also show if an iron tool or weapon had been heated in charcoal to give it a hardened cutting edge. Metalworking in ancient times could be surprisingly sophisticated. This ceremonial bronze axe was from the Mediterranean island of Crete, and was chemically dated to around 3000 BC.

NEUTRON DETECTIVES

Neutron activation analysis can tell archaeologists exactly what something is made of and how and where it was made. Gamma rays are released by bombarding an artefact with neutrons. These rays are then measured to reveal crucial information. For example, fineware ceramics (*right*) found at the Nazca site of Marcaya in Peru, were examined using this technique to find out if they had been made by the native population. It was found that they were produced in a number of different ways, and could not have been produced at Marcaya.

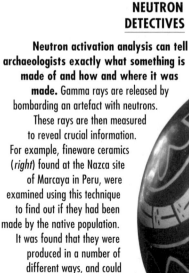

COMPUTERS & ARTEFACTS

Here, an archaeologist is using a grid to study one of the Easter Island statues. The information gathered is fed into a computer to produce a 3D image which can be examined at a later stage. Technology is revolutionizing this side of archaeology. There are now portable laser plotters that allow archaeologists to work quickly in the field, and take home incredibly accurate information.

RECONSTRUCTIONS

To learn more about artefacts, archaeologists sometimes try to recreate them in the way they would have been made traditionally. Archaeologists have refitted flint blades to the stones from which they were struck to find out how the tools were made. The complexity of the process has shown that these tools were made by quite sophisticated people.

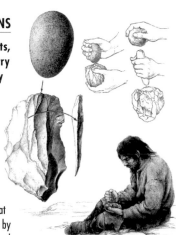

SCIENCE EXPLAINED: DATING POTTERY

Pottery pieces are probably the most plentiful artefacts available to archaeologists. Over time they steadily absorb radioactive elements. When heated to 500 degrees or more, these elements begin to escape in the form of a light energy known as thermoluminescence. To work out when a piece of pottery was fired, archaeologists reheat a sample to measure the amount of light energy within. A formula is then used to convert the amount into a date. This process can date objects up to 80,000 years old.

DISCOVERING HUMAN EVOLUTION

FOOTPRINTS FROM THE PAST

Our earliest ancestor was an ape-like hominid called Australopithecus. In 1974, excavations in northern Ethiopia revealed the most complete Australopithecus skeleton ever found. The team named the skeleton Lucy after the Beatles song, Lucy in the Sky with Diamonds. Then, in 1978, archaeologists discovered some fossilized Australopithecus footprints in northern Tanzania, that were even older than Lucy. They were 3.8 million years old. Two individuals, both estimated at being shorter than five feet, had been walking together, upright, in an environment similar to the one in the main image.

Fossil bones and other traces suggest that the forerunners of human beings seem to have originated in Africa three to four million years ago. Modern man and his ancestors are classified as *hominids*. *Australopithecus* was the first *hominid*, succeeded by *Homo habilis*, then *Homo erectus*. Early modern humans (*Homo sapiens*) appeared in Africa over 100,000 years ago, and then spread out over the world. In Europe and parts of Asia, later modern humans (*Homo sapiens*) encountered another, slightly different type of human being. These we call *Neanderthal*, and they disappeared around 30,000 years ago.

THE *NEANDERTHAL* MYSTERY

Archaeologists are trying to work out why the *Neanderthals* disappeared. In some parts of Europe they may simply have been replaced by the cleverer modern human immigrants; in others they might have been killed off by the newcomers. Elsewhere they may have interbred with modern humans and so merged with them — the skeleton of a young child has been found with both *Neanderthal* and modern human traits.

SCIENCE EXPLAINED: NEW THEORIES

Between 1998 and 1999, archaeologists working in Kenya discovered a fossil skull, jaws and teeth some 3.5 million years old. They are as old as the skeleton of Lucy (Australopithecus), but they are very different in appearance. Archaeologists named this new species Kenyanthropus. The tooth size and face shape of the new find indicate that it had a different diet from Lucy, which suggests that these two species could have co-existed without competing with each other for food. The find throws scientific theories of human evolution into doubt, as previously it had been thought that humans all evolved from a single common ancestor.

HOMO ERECTUS

***Homo erectus* first appeared 1.8 million years ago.** Powerfully built, studies have indicated that *Homo erectus* may have been more efficient at walking than modern humans, whose skeletons have had to adapt to allow for the birth of larger-brained babies. *Homo erectus* skeletons have been found outside Africa, in Asia and Europe. There is evidence that *Homo erectus* probably used fire, and their stone tools are more sophisticated than those of *Homo habilis*.

HOMO HABILIS

Archaeologists have found a number of skulls of *Homo habilis*, which have been dated to 2.4 million years ago. *Homo habilis* is often referred to as 'handy man', because of evidence of tools found with its remains. The average brain size is also considerably larger than in *Australopithecus*, and from making castes, archaeologists have concluded that the brain shape is also more human-like. The area of the brain essential for speech is visible in one brain cast, indicating that *Homo habilis* was possibly capable of basic speech.

HOMO SAPIENS: MODERN MAN

Modern man first appeared about 120,000 years ago. Brain casts show these humans had a much larger brain capacity than earlier hominids, which facilitate reasoning and abstract thought. About 40,000 years ago, tool kits became much more sophisticated, using a wider variety of raw materials such as bone and antler. There were also new implements for engraving, sculpting and making clothing.

STONE SIGNPOSTS?

Numerous boulders on wild moors in northern England and Scotland contain abstract carvings that are thought to date back to the Bronze Age. Archaeologists have noted that many occur on prehistoric routes that were used by Stone Age hunters and also perhaps pilgrims on their way to worship at moorland stone circles. This example (*above*) was discovered on the Isle of Westray in Scotland.

SHIPS OF THE DEAD

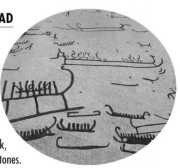

There are many Bronze and Iron Age carvings on rock surfaces in Norway and Sweden. A common, recurring design is that of a ship. By comparing the art with other artefacts, archaeologists have been able to work out that the image symbolized death. At Oseburg in Norway, a massive ship burial was discovered, while in the Viking cemetery at Lindhol Høje in Denmark, there are almost 700 ship-shaped stone gravestones.

THE FIRST WRITING

The Sumerians invented writing, making standardized marks on clay tablets. Called cuneiform, archaeologists learned how to decipher it over the middle decades of the 19th century using other ancient Persian texts. Many of the thousands of clay tablets turned out to be records concerning livestock, temple offerings and trade items. Around the same time as cuneiform was being deciphered, French scholar Jean Francois Champollion deciphered ancient Egyptian hieroglyphic writing by his study of the Rosetta Stone, discovered in Egypt in 1799. It was covered with a text written in three different types of writing – Greek, demotic and hieroglyphic. Because Greek and demotic writing was understood, Champollion was able to work out the meaning of the hieroglyphic text.

DECIPHERING ANCIENT PAINTINGS & WRITINGS

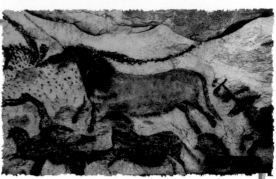

Ancient rock art and writings provide an exciting insight into the imagination and thoughts of past civilizations. Deciphering and interpreting such finds has engaged generations of archaeologists. They often reveal a lot about the society of the time.

EARLY ARTISTS

Paintings found in caves such as Lascaux in France and Altamira in Spain date back around 30,000 years. Although initially archaeologists claimed they were simply decorative, we know that not to be true as most caves are pitch black! Another theory is that the paintings were a form of hunting magic; the artists painted animals they wanted to catch in order to bring them good luck. A final, perhaps more credible theory emerged when it was revealed that these areas supported more people than had been previously imagined. Places like the Lascaux cave may have been places of celebration where marriages and other festivities were held.

KEEPING A RECORD

Bullas were early counting systems made out of clay. They have been found on sites in northern Mesopotamia in Egypt dating from about 8,000 years ago. Bullas consisted of a main clay ball with holes, and similarly-shaped tokens, which could be posted into the bulla. When full, the bulla was closed and stamped with a seal.

MYSTERY CHAPEL

This is the round window of the rock-cut chapel in Externsteine, Germany. It faces the northeastern horizon where two peaks mark the positions of midsummer sunrise and moonrise respectively at a point in the lunar cycle called the 'major standstill', which occurs only every 18.6 years. The chapel was either early Christian or an earlier pagan shrine.

WINTER SUN

The long passage of the great Irish neolithic passage tomb of Newgrange opens towards the rising midwinter sun. On the shortest day of the year, sunbeams penetrate the inner chamber, causing its stones to glow like gold, perhaps bringing the promise of summer and rebirth in the dark depths of winter.

ARCHAEOLOGISTS & ANCIENT ASTRONOMY

The modern study of the use of astronomy by ancient peoples is known as 'archaeoastronomy'. It began around the end of the 19th century, when scientist Sir Norman Lockyer calculated that the axis of Stonehenge had been directed towards midsummer sunrise. In the 20th century, further archaeoastronomical research identified many ancient sites around the world that align with the sun, moon, Venus and stars like Polaris (the north or pole star) or Sirius (the brightest star). It is thought that ancient astronomy was used mainly for ceremonial rather than for scientific purposes.

HEAVENLY WINDOWS

This mysterious building in southern Arizona was used over 700 years ago by the Hohokam Indians. Now called Casa Grande, it may have been an observatory for maintaining the ceremonial calendar. Archaeologists have discovered that the square window at the top right of this picture aligns to the southernmost setting position of the moon, and the round window on the left to the midsummer sunset.

PLANNING STONEHENGE

Stonehenge was meticulously planned to tie in with the rise and fall of the sun and moon. Its architects constructed the circle so that, on midsummer's morning, the sun rose directly over the Heel Stone. The first rays would shine into the centre of the monument through the open arms of the horseshoe stones (*see inset right*).

THE AUBREY HOLES

Archaeoastronomists believe the Aubrey Holes can be used to track the movement of the moon. By moving a marker by two holes every day, a complete cycle of the moon is completed in the time it takes to do a circuit of Stonehenge. It is also argued that the Holes can be used to predict eclipses. Moving a marker three holes a year, it takes the same amount of time to complete a circuit of the stones as it does for the sun to come into alignment with the moon – 18.6 years.

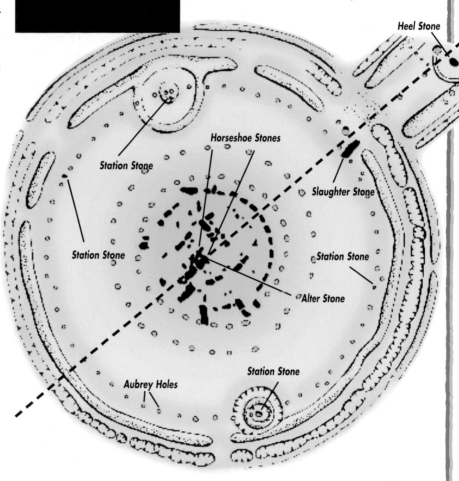

Heel Stone

Horseshoe Stones

Station Stone

Slaughter Stone

Station Stone

Station Stone

Alter Stone

Station Stone

Aubrey Holes

VIKING DWELLINGS

The Sagas also give us some idea of what Viking houses would have looked like. They speak of simple buildings made out of turf and stone. By comparing these descriptions with ruins found in Scandinavia and Northern Europe, archaeologists have been able to build up a detailed picture of Viking houses. Ordinary people lived in single-storey houses with walls made from stone or vertically split tree-trunks (staves), and roofed with thatch or turf (*right*).

IN FROM THE COLD

The Icelandic Sagas were narratives belonging to the medieval Norwegian settlers of the island of Iceland (*above*). The Vikings were intrepid explorers who were constantly in search of new lands. The Viking explorations to Britain and northern Europe, and the journeys to Greenland and beyond, were all written down in these 9th-century texts. What fascinated archaeologists for centuries was the mention of a settlement called 'Vinland', rumoured to be in North America. The Sagas speak of colonies founded by Thorfinn Karlsefni and Leif Ericsson. Using these ancient books as their main source, archaeologists set out to discover if the Vikings really reached the Americas some five centuries before Christopher Columbus.

ANCIENT BOOKS & THE PAST: THE VIKINGS

Old documents, particularly texts, can sometimes yield clues for the archaeologist. The Vikings or Norsemen ('men from the north') came from Norway, Sweden and Denmark, and were at their most powerful between the 8th–11th century. Crucial information about their lifestyles, beliefs and even how far they travelled can be discovered from reading ancient Icelandic texts called the Sagas.

IN THE BOOK

The Sagas contain simple illustrations, offering clues as to what Viking warriors would have worn. When these images are combined with fragments of clothing and helmets found, it is possible to draw up a more accurate picture of how Vikings would have dressed (*below*). Clothing would have been simple and loose-fitting, while helmets were simple in design, not the elaborate, horned helmets that are popularly associated with Viking warriors.

DISCOVERING VINLAND

In the 1960s, Norwegian explorer Helge Ingstad attempted to recreate the voyage westwards from Greenland described in the Sagas. Eventually, he reached the northern Newfoundland coast, and a rectangular group of humps and ridges at a place called L'Anse aux Meadows. The remains of eight turf-walled buildings were uncovered. The largest house had walls 2 metres (6 feet) thick, six rooms and stone hearths. A stone spindle whorl (a woman's spinning tool) proved that European women had been present at the site. Radiocarbon dating identified the settlement as belonging to the early 11th century. It had been a Viking outpost.

SCIENCE EXPLAINED: DECIPHERING LANGUAGE

Archaeologists turned to language specialists in their attempts to track down the legendary 'Vinland' mentioned in the Sagas. One expert suggested that the word 'vin' means meadows, and that the North American Viking settlement was named after its rich meadows. Others suggested that 'vin' referred to grapes, pointing to the fact that grapes are mentioned in the Sagas. However, vines cannot be grown at L'Anse aux Meadow, where the settlement was found, and the earliest editions of the Sagas do not mention grapes. More recently, however, Birgitta Wallace, who was in charge of the excavations at L'Anse aux Meadows, pinpointed an area called New Brunswick, south of the site, where grapes could grow. She suggests that the Vikings named the entire region they explored after this site.

UNDERWATER ARCHAEOLOGY

Air balloon

Underwater archaeology has been used for exploring ancient wells and pools, sunken harbours, drowned cities and ancient shipwrecks. Underwater finds are like time capsules for archaeologists, as organic material tends to survive longer underwater than in air. Recent technological advances have enabled underwater archaeology to make great progress, as discoveries such as *The Mary Rose* illustrate.

UNDER THE WATER

Submersibles and robot submarines allow archaeologists to survey a site both in person, and from the safety of the surface. Once a site has been detected, divers wearing aqualungs can investigate. Before any excavation work begins, a 3D grid is placed around a wreck. Underwater lances and suction pipes are then used to clear away any debris and sediment. Any finds are then carefully mapped by underwater archaeologists using the grid. Special excavation techniques have also been developed to move artefacts. Underwater balloons, for example, can be used to lift heavy objects to the surface.

Robotic craft

3D grid

SCIENCE EXPLAINED: UNDERWATER SURVEY

When surveying a submerged site or wreck, archaeologists tow various kinds of geophysical sensors behind a boat. Proton magnetometers can detect iron and steel objects (like cannon balls and steel hulls), while side-scan sonar can be used to produce a graphic image of features lying on the seabed. Archaeologists can also use sound to search for artefacts. Sub-bottom profilers emit acoustic pulses that can detect objects beneath the surface of the seabed.

SAVING *THE MARY ROSE*

In 1982, the Tudor warship *The Mary Rose* was raised from the seabed, having lain on the ocean floor since 1545. The ship was towed into Portsmouth naval base, wrapped in protective foam and polythene, and constantly sprayed to keep her wet. She was housed in a dry dock providing the right atmosphere for her preservation. About half the starboard (right-hand) side had been preserved, along with some of the decks. An idea of the sailors' diet has been gained from the study of sediments and bones recovered during the excavation. Dried or salted cod were found in baskets, plus mutton, venison and fresh fruit (indicated by a basket of plum stones). Carpentry tools and a medicine chest were also discovered. Overall, the finds on the ship indicated that sailors of the period were relatively well-fed and looked after.

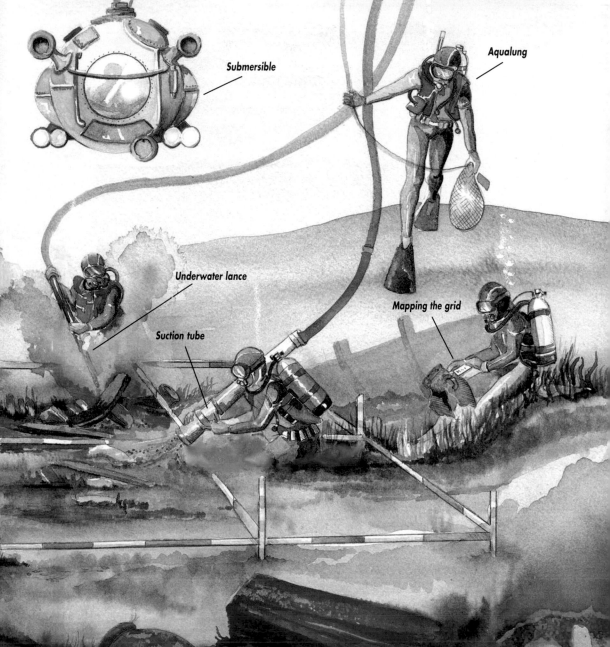

Submersible

Aqualung

Underwater lance

Suction tube

Mapping the grid

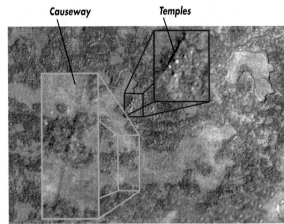

UNDER THE CANOPY

The dense tropical rainforests of Costa Rica (*above*) were long thought to be hiding archaeological remains. In 1985, NASA initiated two flights over the tropical rainforests in the Arenal region in Costa Rica in search of archaeological remains. Linear features were picked up by colour infra-red photographs. Using Landsat photographs and a thermal infra-red scanner to measure the radiation given off the ground, these were later shown to be footpaths (*right*), the oldest in the world, dating from 500 BC. The footpaths were networks of human activity, and much evidence of that activity was later found along them.

Ancient footpath

- ■ Forest
- ■ Deforested
- ■ Water
- ■ Wetland
- ■ Forest Change 1990–93
- ■ Forest Change 1993–95

Causeway   *Temples*

THREATENED HERITAGE

Before the collapse of the Mayan empire in the 9th century AD, the Peten area of Guatemala was inhabited by millions of Maya. Within a few decades, they had all vanished, leaving behind dramatic architecture. Today, the area is being threatened by human activity. Landsat images (*above left*) reveal the extent of deforestation in the Peten. Archaeologists are making use of the same technology to discover sites before they are destroyed. Because vegetation grows in a particular way around ancient ruins, and because ancient Mayan buildings are elevated features in a jungle area that is predominately flat, the Landsat images were able to highlight potential archaeological sites. Archaeologists spotted a causeway and temples (*above right*) among the thick forest.

ARCHAEOLOGY FROM SPACE

Prehistoric roads

Sometimes it is not always possible to see what is going on from the ground. Rugged environments like rainforests are often too dense for archaeologists to explore properly on foot, and discoveries are left mainly to chance. Today, however, using remote sensing equipment such as Landsat satellites and thermal and infra-red scanners, it is possible to explore such areas from above. Pioneered by NASA, these advanced technologies can penetrate darkness, cloud cover and even thick jungle canopies.

CHACO CANYON

Between AD 900–1100, an ancient people called the Anasazi settled Chaco Canyon, New Mexico, and left behind evidence of a highly sophisticated society (*below*). In 1982, NASA's archaeological research committee carried out a search for ancient roads, using remote sensing technology. Although scientists and archaeologists alike were sceptical that the technology would be successful, the results were stunning. The thermal infra-red scanner, which measures temperature differences near the ground, picked up over 320 km (200 miles) of roads, ancient buildings and agricultural fields (*above*).

Chaco Canyon ruins

SCIENCE EXPLAINED: GROUND TRUTHING

While remote sensing can provide archaeologists with invaluable clues as to where archaeological sites may lie, this technology does not eliminate the need for someone on the ground to verify this information. This process is called ground truthing. When ruins are revealed by aerial techniques, teams of archaeologists set out on foot to investigate.

DEBUNKING MYSTERIES

Sometimes the biggest challenge for archaeologists is searching out the truth. Many 'ancient' artefacts may not be quite what they seem, while others have been attributed mystical, supernatural qualities. Through time-consuming research and the use of the latest scientific techniques, archaeologists have been able to separate the true puzzles of the past from bogus mysteries.

LEYLINES

In 1921, English businessman Alfred Watkins claimed that ancient sites fell into straight lines across the landscape called 'leys'. He thought they were prehistoric traders' tracks, and claimed churches had evolved on certain marker points along the leys. In the 1960s, people rediscovered his theory, and called the lines 'leylines'. They fantasized that they were channels of some mysterious energy. Aerial surveys since Watkins's time have discredited his theory. Most of the leys were chance alignments, but some resulted from medieval funeral paths leading to old churches. The ancient track shown here leads to Llanthony Abbey in the Welsh mountains.

ATLANTEAN AMERICA?

Atlantis enthusiasts feel that the presence of ancient pyramids in both Egypt and the Americas is proof that survivors from the fabled lost land in the Atlantic Ocean must have spread east and west. However, the design of the pyramids in the Americas is, in fact, quite different to that of the Egyptian pyramids. Moreover, Mayan pyramids in Mexico are over 3,000 years younger than the Egyptian versions! Shown here is a Mayan stepped pyramid at Chichen Itza.

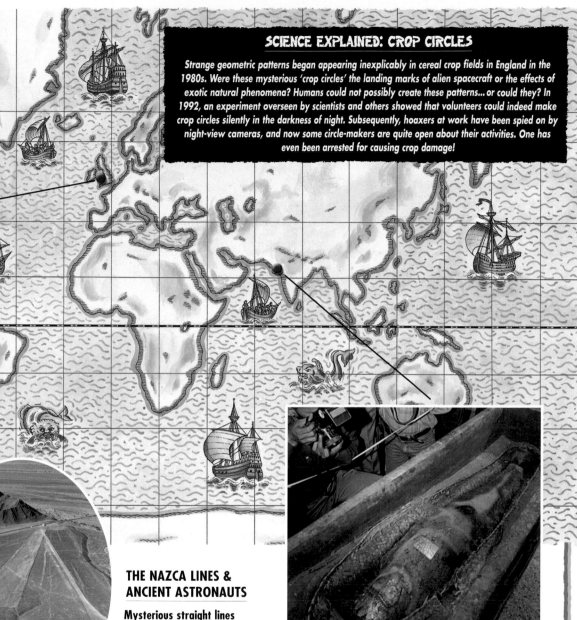

Strange geometric patterns began appearing inexplicably in cereal crop fields in England in the 1980s. Were these mysterious 'crop circles' the landing marks of alien spacecraft or the effects of exotic natural phenomena? Humans could not possibly create these patterns... or could they? In 1992, an experiment overseen by scientists and others showed that volunteers could indeed make crop circles silently in the darkness of night. Subsequently, hoaxers at work have been spied on by night-view cameras, and now some circle-makers are quite open about their activities. One has even been arrested for causing crop damage!

THE NAZCA LINES & ANCIENT ASTRONAUTS

Mysterious straight lines and other markings on desert areas around Nazca, Peru, have provoked much speculation. Some people claim these 'Nazca lines' were the runways of extra-terrestrial craft.

The desert markings are certainly remarkable, but ancient spacemen are not the answer. They are easily made by removing the darkened surface of the desert to reveal a lighter subsoil – indeed, the desert surface is so sensitive even footprints can remain for centuries! Researchers now feel they relate to strange religious practices of prehistoric American Indians.

FAKE MUMMIES

In October 2000, it was announced on Pakistani national television that a 2,600-year-old mummy found in Kharan had been sold to the National Museum in Karachi.

The mummy was wrapped in Egyptian style and was resting in a wooden coffin decorated with cuneiform writing and images (*see page 12*). However, when fully translated the cuneiform turned out to be a direct copy of a previously discovered inscription. A cuneiform expert revealed the inscription dated from no earlier than the 1930s. A full-body scan of the mummy confirmed suspicions. It revealed the corpse to be that of a 21-year-old woman who was mummified less than two years ago.

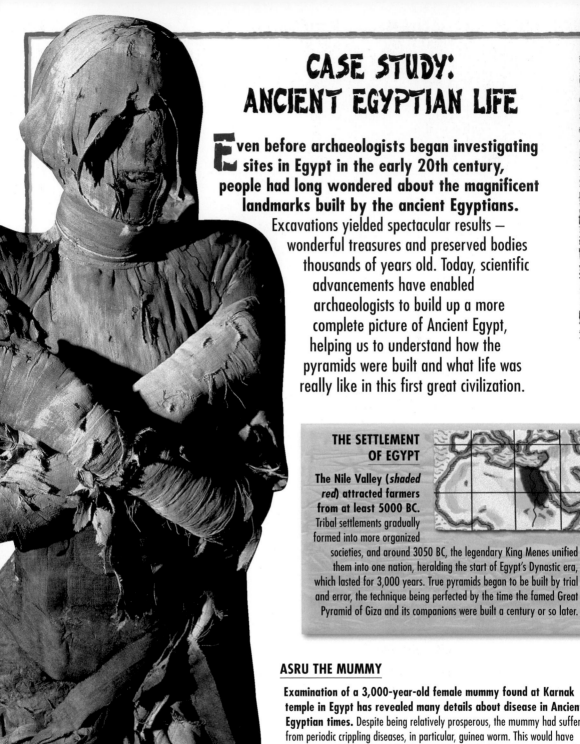

CASE STUDY:
ANCIENT EGYPTIAN LIFE

Even before archaeologists began investigating sites in Egypt in the early 20th century, people had long wondered about the magnificent landmarks built by the ancient Egyptians. Excavations yielded spectacular results — wonderful treasures and preserved bodies thousands of years old. Today, scientific advancements have enabled archaeologists to build up a more complete picture of Ancient Egypt, helping us to understand how the pyramids were built and what life was really like in this first great civilization.

THE SETTLEMENT OF EGYPT

The Nile Valley (*shaded red***) attracted farmers from at least 5000 BC.** Tribal settlements gradually formed into more organized societies, and around 3050 BC, the legendary King Menes unified them into one nation, heralding the start of Egypt's Dynastic era, which lasted for 3,000 years. True pyramids began to be built by trial and error, the technique being perfected by the time the famed Great Pyramid of Giza and its companions were built a century or so later.

ASRU THE MUMMY

Examination of a 3,000-year-old female mummy found at Karnak temple in Egypt has revealed many details about disease in Ancient Egyptian times. Despite being relatively prosperous, the mummy had suffered from periodic crippling diseases, in particular, guinea worm. This would have caused intestinal bleeding and diarrhoea. Her legs had been amputated just before her death, suggesting that they were heavily ulcerated as a result of trying to scratch out the worms. Her lungs were filled with sand, which tell us that she would have had great trouble breathing. X-rays tell us that she had arthritis in her hands and osteoarthritis in her back. No traces of any painkillers were found on the body, although it is known that the blue lotus flower was used to help improve blood circulation, which would have done something to ease the pain.

LIFE FOR THE WORKERS

Recent archaeological work at Giza (*above*) has thrown up some fascinating facts about how the pyramids were built. Inscriptions found in the tombs tell us that large gangs were recruited to build the pyramids, and that they were well organized. Microscopic food residues found at the site reveal that workers were well fed on bread, fish and beef, and decay in tooth specimens has revealed that weak beer and honey were also a substantial part of the diet. Ancient medical kits have been also been found. This new evidence suggests that the workers at the pyramids were treated better than popular opinion suggests.

HOW LONG DID IT TAKE?

The Greek historian Herodotus states in AD 300 that it took 100,000 slaves to build the pyramids. However, an experiment has been carried out to test this theory. Using tools and techniques of the time, as depicted on many engravings (*above*), archaeologists have been able to calculate that a workforce of just 40,000 would have been needed to build the pyramids, in a timespan of 10 years.

HARD GRAFT

DNA analysis on bodies found in one of the worker's pyramids at Giza revealed that they all belonged to family groups. Cut marks on some of the bones reveal that many of the bodies had broken arms, while there was evidence in several cases of limbs being amputated. This suggests that however well the pyramid workers were treated, the work was still back-breaking.

SCIENCE EXPLAINED: THE INTERNATIONAL MUMMY TISSUE BANK

In 1995, Rosalie David, the head of the Manchester Mummy Research Project based in Britain, decided to set up an international tissue bank. She approached around 8,000 institutions around the world to request tissue samples from mummies to add to the bank, with a great deal of success. The DNA samples collected will provide a unique insight into life in Ancient Egypt.

CASE STUDY: OTZI THE ICEMAN

In September 1991, the deep-frozen remains of a 5,000-year-old man were found high in the Otzal Alps on the Italy-Austria border. Forensic science and pathological examination have provided archaeologists with a wealth of information about this man, nicknamed 'Otzi', recreating his last steps and telling us much about his lifestyle, diet and how he died.

BIRCH FUNGUS

In Otzi's backpack there were pieces of birch fungus. It is likely that the fungus was part of Otzi's medical kit, because the birch fungus contains antibiotic substances, and it is effective against various bacteria, including those causing tuberculosis. It was also considered to be a powerful medicine in ancient Greece.

BONE DEGENERATION

Tattoo marks were found on Otzi's body, in areas which the autopsy showed to be suffering from bone degeneration (his spine area, right knee and both ankles). It seems likely that the tattoos were part of a pain-relieving treatment. In folk medicine, it is a widespread belief that tattooing can help alleviate joint and muscle pains.

WEAPONRY

When he died, Otzi was carrying a bow and a quiverful of arrows. Although he had been carrying a dozen arrow shafts, only two were ready for use. His quiver was also damaged. Archaeologists think he was in the process of repairing it, and that he had been recently involved in a skirmish. In his injured condition, he had been forced to make the dangerous journey over the mountains — a journey he was never to complete.

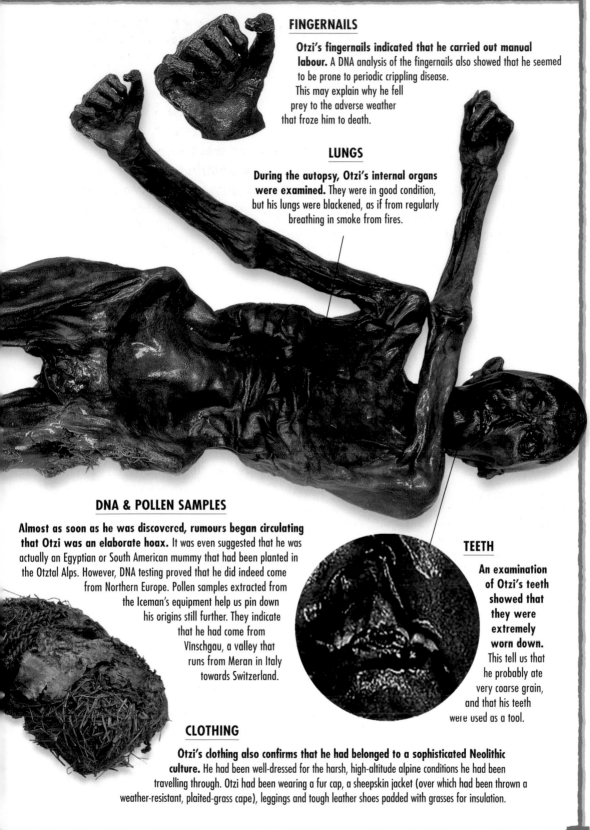

FINGERNAILS

Otzi's fingernails indicated that he carried out manual labour. A DNA analysis of the fingernails also showed that he seemed to be prone to periodic crippling disease. This may explain why he fell prey to the adverse weather that froze him to death.

LUNGS

During the autopsy, Otzi's internal organs were examined. They were in good condition, but his lungs were blackened, as if from regularly breathing in smoke from fires.

DNA & POLLEN SAMPLES

Almost as soon as he was discovered, rumours began circulating that Otzi was an elaborate hoax. It was even suggested that he was actually an Egyptian or South American mummy that had been planted in the Otztal Alps. However, DNA testing proved that he did indeed come from Northern Europe. Pollen samples extracted from the Iceman's equipment help us pin down his origins still further. They indicate that he had come from Vinschgau, a valley that runs from Meran in Italy towards Switzerland.

TEETH

An examination of Otzi's teeth showed that they were extremely worn down. This tell us that he probably ate very coarse grain, and that his teeth were used as a tool.

CLOTHING

Otzi's clothing also confirms that he had belonged to a sophisticated Neolithic culture. He had been well-dressed for the harsh, high-altitude alpine conditions he had been travelling through. Otzi had been wearing a fur cap, a sheepskin jacket (over which had been thrown a weather-resistant, plaited-grass cape), leggings and tough leather shoes padded with grasses for insulation.

CASE STUDY: POMPEII

On 24th August AD 79, the Roman city of Pompeii was buried under a deluge of ash and lava as the volcano Vesuvius vented its anger on the region. Although it was a catastrophe for the city, it was a gift to archaeologists of later generations. Pompeii was sealed and almost perfectly preserved by the lava, left untouched until the 18th century. Early efforts at excavating the site were haphazard, and the ruins were plundered for treasures. In 1860, under the direction of the Italian archaeologist Guiseppe Fiorelli, systematic excavation and restoration work began. Today, modern Pompeii (*pictured below*) is built around the ancient city.

DAILY LIFE

The ruins of Pompeii give us many clues as to what life might have been like for inhabitants of the city at the time of the eruption. Mosaics and paintings on the walls of houses depict life in the town. Writings on the walls also give information on the price of goods, together with the likes and dislikes of the population. Pompeii was a busy port town, full of shops, restaurants and residential areas. The poor often lived in rooms above shops, while the rich lived in enormous houses with beautiful courtyard gardens.

SCIENCE EXPLAINED: PRESERVING THE EVIDENCE

In AD 79, pumice and ash blown out by Vesuvius buried the bodies of Pompeii citizens. The ash hardened around the bodies, forming moulds. As the bodies decayed, eventually only hollow shells were left. Guiseppe Fiorelli came up with a way to recreate the bodies of the Pompeii victims from these casts. He recreated the bodies by making small holes in the hardened ash and pouring in plaster of Paris. When the plaster hardened, Fiorelli chipped away the ash to reveal a perfect cast of the body (left).

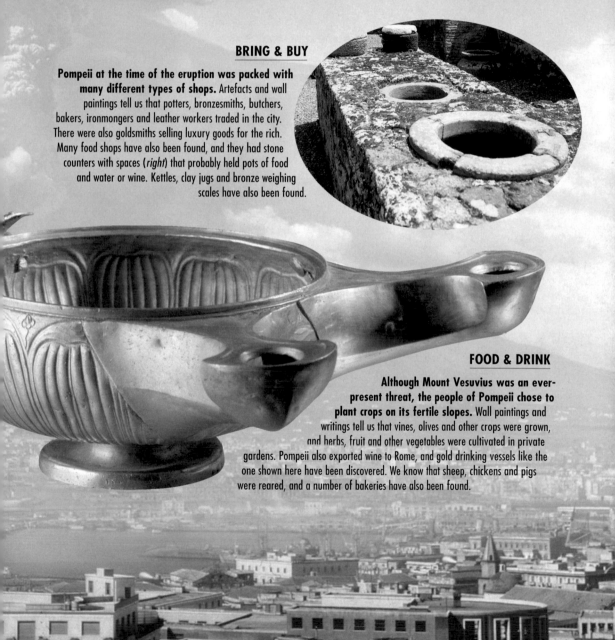

CULTURE

Archaeological evidence tells us the city boasted two theatres, one of which was big enough to seat up to 5,000 people. Mosaics show actors wearing masks and stage costume, and the writings on the walls tell us how much the people enjoyed the theatre. Another popular element of life were the gladiatorial combats which took place at the amphitheatre. Shows ranged from gladiatorial combats to fights between wild animals. Helmets, shin protectors and ankle guards have been found, and scribings on walls tell us that gladiators were often hero-worshipped by the citizens of Pompeii.

BRING & BUY

Pompeii at the time of the eruption was packed with many different types of shops. Artefacts and wall paintings tell us that potters, bronzesmiths, butchers, bakers, ironmongers and leather workers traded in the city. There were also goldsmiths selling luxury goods for the rich. Many food shops have also been found, and they had stone counters with spaces (*right*) that probably held pots of food and water or wine. Kettles, clay jugs and bronze weighing scales have also been found.

FOOD & DRINK

Although Mount Vesuvius was an ever-present threat, the people of Pompeii chose to plant crops on its fertile slopes. Wall paintings and writings tell us that vines, olives and other crops were grown, and herbs, fruit and other vegetables were cultivated in private gardens. Pompeii also exported wine to Rome, and gold drinking vessels like the one shown here have been discovered. We know that sheep, chickens and pigs were reared, and a number of bakeries have also been found.

ARMCHAIR ARCHAEOLOGY

By using computer-aided design (CAD) software, it is now possible to take a virtual tour through an archaeological site. A computer is fed with a dense array of digitized data obtained during an excavation to enable it to literally recreate the past. Hadrian's Baths were a Roman bathing complex constructed at Leptis Magma in AD 120. Using data extracted from examining the ruins of the site (*above*), a reconstructed flythrough of the Baths has been created (*right*).

BRINGING THE PAST TO LIFE

Living museums offer visitors an altogether more interactive experience of the past. The Weald and Downland Open Air Museum in England is a collection of 40 historical buildings dating from the 14th century, which have been rescued from destruction. Each building was carefully dismantled from its original site, conserved and then rebuilt at the Museum. The interiors were recreated in the style of the period, and archaeologists used written evidence and plant samples found at the original sites to faithfully replant the gardens. There is even a working water mill where stone ground flour is produced daily, and a Tudor farm complete with ancient breeds. Around the site, carpenters and tradesmen demonstrate traditional building and craft techniques.

LIVING ARCHAEOLOGY

Archaeology today has been transformed by science, becoming more alive and relevant than ever before. Archaeologists get involved with everything from rescuing and restoring important monuments to enticing people to become more interested in the past. This ranges from the building of living museums to the creation of flythroughs on the Internet that allow people to visit archaeological sites from the comfort of their own homes. Today's archaeologists are also beginning to look at our most recent past, examining industrial artefacts and even our own rubbish to learn about modern life.

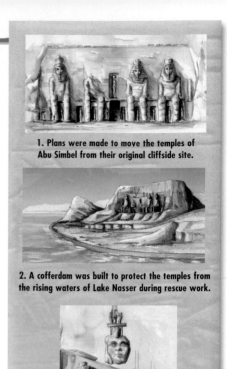

1. Plans were made to move the temples of Abu Simbel from their original cliffside site.

2. A cofferdam was built to protect the temples from the rising waters of Lake Nasser during rescue work.

3. Piece by piece, the temple was dismantled. The heads of Ramses II were cut away and taken to a new location.

ARCHAEOLOGY OF TODAY

Today, archaeologists explore the recent, as well as the distant past.

In the United States, a branch of archaeology called garbage archaeology, has sprung up. Archaeological techniques are used to study the rubbish of modern society, to paint a more accurate picture of life today. At the University of Arizona, Professor Rathje and his team have studied thousands of tons of garbage in order to build up a sophisticated database about American society. It has revealed fascinating facts about diet, the materials we use, and the difference between the rich and poor.

4. Finally, the pieces of Abu Simbel were put back together in their new location.

SALVAGE ARCHAEOLOGY

One of the key roles of archaeologists today is to protect our heritage from damage caused by the environment and human activity. In Egypt, archaeological specialists from all over the world were drafted in to protect archaeological sites along the Nile threatened by a new dam that was to be built in the area. After a comprehensive survey, many temples were dismantled and re-erected in a safer place; some were donated to museums.

GLOSSARY

Archaeobotany – Branch of archaeology that examines ancient plant remains

Archaeoastronomy – Study of the use of astronomy by ancient peoples

Artefacts – Portable objects made by humans

Computer site visualization – The use of computer-aided design packages to create virtual flythroughs of archaeological sites

DNA – Genetic material that contains the blueprint for life

Dendrochronology – The technique of dating by using tree rings

Ecofacts – The remains of living organisms

Ethnoarchaeology – The study of living cultures to understand past cultures

Faunal remains – Skeletons and bone fragments of humans and animals

Features – Static evidence of human activity

Garbage archaeology – The study of rubbish left by modern societies

Gradiometer – Instrument used to measure the gradient of magnetic variations in the ground and pinpoint the locations of clay artefacts

Ground truthing – The verification of remotely-sensed information by archaeologists on the ground

Hominid – A family of primates which includes man and his descendants

Magnometer – Device used to measure magnetic waves under the ground

Metallographic examination – The use of chemical etching to study metal artefacts

Neutron activation analysis – Dating technique which uses gamma rays

Potassium-argon dating – Dating technique that measures the rate of decay of potassium

Radiocarbon dating – Technique that dates remains by studying carbon levels

Remote sensing – Aerial technology used to take pictures of suspected archaeological sites

Resistivity meter – Equipment used to detect variations in underground moisture

Thermoluminescence – Radioactive dating technique used to date flints and pottery

Typological dating – Dating technique that compares styles of artefacts

Uranium-series dating – Dating technique that measures calcium carbonate levels in rocks

ACKNOWLEDGEMENTS

We would like to thank: Advocate and Elizabeth Wiggans for their assistance.
Illustrations by John Alston and Simon Mendez.
Copyright © 2006 *ticktock* Entertainment Ltd.
First published in Great Britain by ticktock Publishing Ltd., Unit 2, Orchard Business Park, North Farm Road, Tunbridge Wells, Kent TN2 3XF. All rights reserved.
No part of this publication may be reproduced, stored in a retrieval system, or transmitted in any form or by any means electronic, mechanical,
photocopying, recording or otherwise, without prior written permission of the copyright owner.
A CIP catalogue record for this book is available from the British Library. ISBN 1 86007 463 4.
Printed in Hong Kong. 123456789

t=top, b=bottom, c=centre, l=left, r=right, OFC=outside front cover, IFC=inside front cover, IBC=inside back cover, OBC=outside back cover

Ancient Art & Architecture Collection: 12-13c, 13t. Corbis Images: OFC, 7c, 9t, 8-9cb & OBC, 17t, 20t, 21b, 23cr, 24l & OBC, 25t, 25r, 28t, 28-29cs, 29t, 29cr, 29c, 30t, 31b.
Paul Devereux: 8b, 14t, 14b, 14-15b, 15t, 22t, 22b. Dr. Richard Hall: 17c. Kobal Collection: 2bl. Mary Rose Trust: 19t. Natural History Picture Agency: 16c.
South American Pictures: 22-23c. Charles Tait: 2tl, 8t, 12t. South Tyroll Museum: 26-27 & OFC. Weald and Downland Open Air Museum: 30b. Werner Forman Archive: 12c, 25c, 28b.

Every effort has been made to trace the copyright holders and we apologize in advance for any unintentional omissions.
We would be pleased to insert the appropriate acknowledgement in any subsequent edition of this publication.

snapping-turtle
guide